Irregardless

And Other Grammar Error's Too Irritate and Annoy

Look hard to find the grammer errors

Allison I. Williams

And

Kenneth J. Williams

ISBN-13: 978-1481970297

ISBN-10: 1481970291

DEDICATION

Too Bob, whom is won of the people I could allways share bad grammar
stories with. My favorite phone call's from him were storie's about
interview's and resume's that he collected over the year's
I can't look at frozen pipe's the same.

And two Jan, who's insistance on the use of proper grammar has allways
been a source of entertainment for me.

CONTENT'S

ACKNOWLEDGMENT'S

Irregardless of what I say, I appreciate the people in my life who push me to do things. Sometimes they push me harder than I want, but when there idea's are good one's, I have to follow through.

Allison and me started talking about this book some time ago, and we finally realized that we could make it a reality. Allison is my daughter, and this project has been a great way for us to have fun together.

We are especially thankful to Alisons cousin (who is coincidentally my niece), Kate Watson, who know's the pet peeve's of her English teacher, who is also her grandmother (and my mother-in-law), Jan. You have brought a great deal of joy to our live's.

--Ken Williams

CHAPTER ONE

IRREGARDLESS OF WHAT YOU THINK, *IRREGARDLESS* IS A WORD

"Irregardless isn't a word." That's what the English snobs insist, and they self-righteously cite history and tradition to prove their point. They may even invoke the wisdom of the omnipotent Microsoft corporation, which has deemed it appropriate to put the red squiggly underline beneath the word, suggesting that the word may be misspelled.

Irregardless of what Microsoft thinks, I like the word *Irregardless*. I right-click on the alleged error, and the two choices I have are "Regardless" and "I Regardless." No, I don't like those choices.

Irregardless of the persistent insistence of my critics, I contend that *irregardless* is a word. It's a mighty fine word. How can it not be a word? How can we settle this like civilized people?

Perhaps you will suggest that I should look up the word in the dictionary. I have, though it's probably not the word you were expecting. I looked up "word." What is a "word?" As far as I can tell, a "word" is a unit of language that functions as a carrier of meaning.

When I say *irregardless*, do you know what I mean? Do you understand that I mean the same thing that I would mean if I had said *regardless*? Of course you do. The letters that make up the word *irregardless* convey a meaning. It is a word.

I must confess that I am one of those English snobs who thinks that irregardless of the lazy word choice of a growing contingent of the English-speaking world, the corruption of the language must be stilled. That is one of my guiding principles. However, and unfortunately for the rest of the purists, a deeper guiding principle in my life is this: If it bugs my mother-in-law and entertains me in the process, I must do it.

CHAPTER TOO

PROPER USE OF APOSTROPHE'S IS NOT ROCKET SURGERY

To understand how to correctly use apostrophe's, you must first understand the history of apostrophe's.

The apostrophe was invented by an Italian-American named Clarke Apostrophe in the year 1722. He suffered from sickle cell anemia, which coincidentally, was also invented that same year. Clarke was looking at a blood sample through the microscope, and he realized that half the red blood cells formed commas, and the other half formed the same shape, but they were much higher on the line. He decided to call them Apostrophe's and he petitioned the Italian-American government to require their use in all plural's. For some reason, however, the use of apostrophe's has become confusing for some.

Apostrophe's should not be that hard to figure out. For some reason, though, it seem's that a growing number of the worlds youth are misusing apostrophe's. Really? Come on, guy's. It is not rocket surgery.

The actual rule's of when to use apostrophe's are too complex and confusing. The best rule of thumb is to slap apostrophe's at the end of any word that ends with "s."

If you have one cookie, and I have one cookie, together we have two cookie's. I have two sister's and three brother's. I have one dog and two cat's.

See? It is simple.

The grammar Nazi's will insist that apostrophe's are being misused. I think I understand, but it is for a good cause. AOL will donate five cent's to help cure sickle cell anemia, in memory of Clarke, for each apostrophe that is posted on a facebook status or is sent in text message's. So, it is all for a good cause.

CHAPTER THREE

YOUR RIGHT IF YOU THINK YOU'RE GRAMMAR MATTERS

Since your reading this book, your probably hoping to improve you're grammar skill's. Trust me. You're writing will never be the same if you follow the tip's that I outline in these chapter's Your likely to become well-known in you're circle of friend's, and you're boss will probably use you as an example to you're coworker's.

Most of what we communicate to each other is non-verbal. You're word's matter. The way you put you're word's together is critical in whether you're message is received and understood. You're intention's must be clear, so it is important that you're word's are chosen carefully so that you're message is easily understood.

Your probably wondering why grammar is so important. Think about the last time you saw something written with poor grammar. Maybe it was an office memo, or maybe it was a note from the school. If your like me, when you see grammar mistake's, your probably going to assume that the person who wrote the memo is less intelligent than they really are. In fact, statistic's show that serious grammar error's reduced perceived intelligence by 23 point's, on a scale of one to ten. Your not immune from this bias, so you're best bet will be to carefully choose the word's that you use in you're writing. Do not fall into the trap of letting you're audience think your dumber than you are! Proof read you're correspondence, and if you're word processing program's support grammar checking, take advantage of you're technology.

Ken and Allison Williams

CHAPTER FOUR

THEIR READING THERE BOOK OVER THEY'RE

I n this chapter your going to learn that there is a difference between "their," "there," and "they're." There not interchangeable. They're meaning's are different. For example, one is possessive. That mean's that your talking about something that belong's to someone or something. One is a contraction. Not the kind your having when you're baby is born, but the kind that mean's its two word's smashed together. Finally, the third one is a place, like when your describing something that is not here.

Their is lot's of example's that should help you understand the difference. As you're familiarity of the rules of proper grammar improves, you're writing will improve. To simplify you're understanding of the different ways your going to use those three option's, consider these possibilitie's:

There favorite place to go on vacation is California.

They're car is out of gas.

Their going to the park for there family picture's.

There best friend love's elephant's.

We are going over they're.

Their singing there favorite song's over they're.

Their planning they're schedule's for there summer vacation.

Their playing hide-and-seek.

What could be simpler? The most important thing's to remember are that their are difference's between the three word's, and you're task is to understand the message's your trying to communicate. You're word's will be clearly understood by there hearer's.

CHAPTER FIVE

ITS IT'S, NOT ITS

Its surprising to us how frequently the simple word "its," and it's cousin, "it's" are misused. For we master's of the English language, seeing those short, but quite important, word's misused is like fingernail's scraping across a million chalkboard's. But kid's these day's don't even know what a chalkboard is, so its probably better if we were to come up with a better analogy.

Ok. Maybe this will make some sense: Its like grating you're knuckle's with a cheese greater.

Its something that make's us shudder. It hurt's our ear's. Its horrible enough that I don't want to even think about it. Ick.

Its common knowledge that you're average high school student's will have a hard time wanting to learn about there native language, especially if they're native language is English. Without making a sweeping generalization, high school student's these day's are lazy. Their uncommitted to learning there basic grammar rule's. Its because of they're laziness that we felt its important to write this book to clarify the rule's of grammar that their ignoring. When I was they're age, I had two learn grammar rule's. Its because of this that I think its so important for kid's these day's to learn how too speak there language.

Its good too get that off my chest. I didn't intend to turn this book into my own personal soapbox for my own rant's, but its a good opportunity two speak to the youth's of the world.

.

CHAPTER SIX

TAKE A BREATH AND RELAX, SLIP INTO A COMMA.

I realized something, a few weeks ago and I think this chapter, is the right place to share it. I really like writing, long sentence's. Not all, of my sentence's are long mind you but, I seem to like making, long complex sentence's that can, become or could, become confusing if you don't read them the same, way that I wrote them.

Of course comma's, are used to break up long, sentences. This has lead me to undertake, a more serious study of comma's. I remember, being in music classe's when I was much younger when, one of my teacher's tried to help us understand a, unusual, notation that we were seeing, on the page. "When you see the, comma on the music" she told us "that is where, you take a breathe." If that is the only thing, that you gain, from this chapter, I will have, served my purpose well. You should assume, that you're reader's are dumb not in a, rude way but in the way that is not negative. You have to assume, that they don't really understand what you are, writing and if, they can't figure out what you are, talking about surely, they can't be trusted to breathe, on their own. As you write pay close, attention to when you breathe and, put a comma their. The attentive reader, will notice this and follow you're lead. Have you heard of, posture mirroring? For example when your in an, interview some people recommend, that you mirror the posture of the person, who is interviewing, you. This according to, research should help the other person, relax and sense a, subconscious connection to you. When you place you're "breath comma's" as I like, to call them you are doing the, same thing in your, writing. Using comma's this, way is kind of like a, speed bump. You can add, emphasis to an idea, this way. And by you're clever and, intentional use of comma's you're reader's will subconsciously, see the comma take, a breath and they, will begin to match you're respiratory, state that you were in when, you were writing. This will bring the reader and, the author together in an, important and intimate, way. You will be, understood at a deeper and more, personal level. After all, thats what every, good writer want's.

CHAPTER SEVEN

U DNT AV NUF TYM 2 RITE D HOL WRD

W r ll vry bZ ppl. fings r changN fstR thN they hv @ Ny oder pt in humn hx. W d incr of d dmds on r tym, we smply dnt av d tym dat we uzd 2 av. We nd 2 fnd wAz 2 save tym whrvr n whnvr we cn.

1 way 2 save tym S 2 Mbrace d teknoloG dat hs Bcum nown 4 it's advncs n saving tym. We nd 2 strt ritN lk we txt.

TxtN wz slO 2 evolv. N d 80s, cel fons wr vry XpNsiv n dey wr d sIz of smll cottages. Txt msgs wr sent by postal mAl. N dis antiquated sys, it cUd tak ^ 2 7days 2 snd a short "I luv U" txt 2 yr gf or bf!

Fortunatly a real altRntve 4 postal mAl txtN wz invented sumtIm n d 90s, & it hz takN off n d 21st centRe. nErly L cel fone plans hv txtN svcs. EvN my gma text's. WL, she dont, bt a lot uv gma's I knO text, & w txtN comes d nEd 2 b mo clr n d msg's we snd.

TxtN hz adopted a nu std N lngwij. Spelling d hol wrd hz bcum antiquated, & onlE losers spL aL d wrds d way we lrnd 2 n eng claS. & n fact, d letR "U" hz officially bcum recognized az d coRec spelling 4 d wrd

"You." & d # 2 iz nw d propR spelling 4 d wrds formly knwn az "to" o

"too." Ironically, d # "two" iz nw spelled "to."

Som critics sA dat txtN lingo iz hard 2 undRstNd & cn rEzlt n confusion.

I say, git a Lyf. f their's somTIN U dnt undrstnd, ask a 4 Yr O. Trust us.

txtN saves tym & saves lives. ProblE.

CHAPTER EIGHT

IF YOU ASK ME PUNCTUATION IS OVERRATED YOU DONT REALLY NEED TO LEARN HOW TO USE IT.

N ow that I think about it the whole problem with grammar well not really the whole problem but a big part of the problem is that it is very difficult to learn and remember all of the grammar rule's if you look at the chapter's in this book you will see that a couple of chapter's are focused on punctuation wouldnt it be easier if we just did away with punctuation all together and we didnt even address semi colons or when to use explanation points which I call explanation points instead of exclamation points because I think its funnier that way but anyway or is it anyway's I can never remember so I will just use anyway because that will save some of my letters I am allotted only a certain number of esse's that look's weird I think I could say ss or s but Im not sure if you will understand what Im saying but thats not my fault I guess I should start over this chapter has really gotten away from me and for that I apologize.

This book has a specific purpose there are actually two purpose's first as I mentioned in the first chapter I am a grammar purist I think that people should learn the grammar rules of the English language yes they are difficult to remember and yes some of them dont make sense but they are important written language is critical in communicating idea's to individual's and group's of people if you write in an unclear manner the meaning can be misunderstood or misconstrued altogether write clear concise sentence's make sure that the word's you choose convey the meaning that you want to convey make sure to use proper spelling and correct punctuation dont rely on your spell checker to do the thinking for you if you struggle with the language find a friend who can help explain or fix any error's you inadvertently commit with some help you can help rid the world of horrible grammar.

.

ABOUT THE AUTHORS

Surprisingly Ken is an English Language snob and each chapter hurt a
different part of his brain. "Writing wrongly is hard" he said with a wink
knowing that the whole book was written "poorly." He has been married
to the same woman longer than most people in Bolivia have been alive.
Allison is his favorite daughter unless you include his other daughter in
which case Allison is in the top two.

Allison is a contributor and was the inspiration for this book. She has
finally left home for the big adventures in Idaho where she is attending
college for the first time. She is a fan of Batman so if any boys reading this
want to take her out she likes Batman and The Avengers. Her favorite is
when you misquote movie lines.

Made in the USA
Charleston, SC
16 July 2013